Animal 911
ENVIRONMENTAL THREATS

Animals on the Verge of Extinction

KAREN O'CONNOR

Gareth Stevens
Publishing

Please visit our website, www.garethstevens.com
For a free color catalog of all our high-quality books,
call toll free 1-800-542-2595 or fax 1-877-542-2596.

Library of Congress Cataloging-in-Publication Data

O'Connor, Karen.
Animals on the verge of extinction / by Karen O'Connor.
 p. cm. — (Animal 911: environmental threats)
Includes index.
ISBN 978-1-4339-9715-0 (pbk.)
ISBN 978-1-4339-9716-7 (6-pack)
ISBN 978-1-4339-9714-3 (library binding)
1. Endangered species—Juvenile literature. 2. Wildlife conservation—Juvenile literature. I. Title.
QL83.O35 2014
591.68—dc23

Published in 2014 by
Gareth Stevens Publishing
111 East 14th Street, Suite 349
New York, NY 10003

© 2014 Gareth Stevens Publishing

Produced by Planman Technologies
Designed by Sandy Kent
Edited by Jon Bogart

Contents

Words in the glossary appear in **bold** type the first time they are used in the text.

What Is Extinction?

How would you like to see:

– A flock of passenger pigeons so large it blackened the sky?

– An animal that looks like it's half zebra and half horse, called a quagga?

– A Tasmanian wolf, a large **carnivorous** marsupial?

Sorry. You can't. They no longer exist. These animals are all **extinct**.

The word *extinct* means the **species** is no longer alive. Some species are close to becoming extinct. They are **endangered**. Scientists watch endangered animals closely so they will not become extinct. Right now, scientists are trying to save the sea turtle, the brown spider monkey, the golden toad, and many other species.

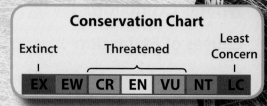

Conservation Chart

Extinct		Threatened				Least Concern
EX	EW	CR	EN	VU	NT	LC

The numbers of rhinoceroses have declined a lot in recent years, leaving them endangered and perhaps on the verge of extinction.

4

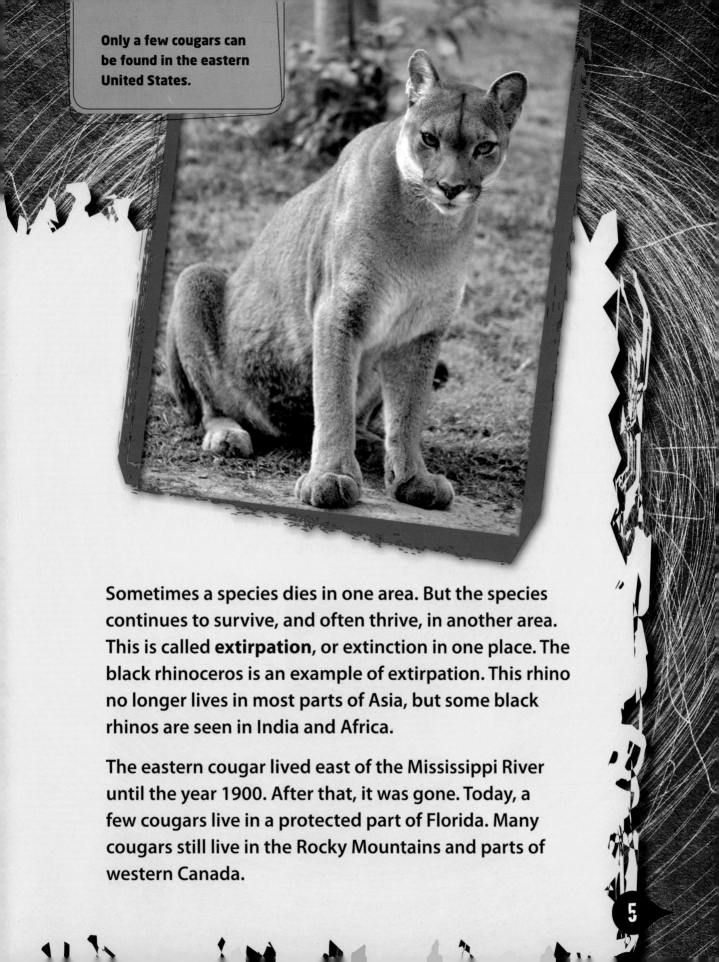

Only a few cougars can be found in the eastern United States.

Sometimes a species dies in one area. But the species continues to survive, and often thrive, in another area. This is called **extirpation**, or extinction in one place. The black rhinoceros is an example of extirpation. This rhino no longer lives in most parts of Asia, but some black rhinos are seen in India and Africa.

The eastern cougar lived east of the Mississippi River until the year 1900. After that, it was gone. Today, a few cougars live in a protected part of Florida. Many cougars still live in the Rocky Mountains and parts of western Canada.

Causes of Extinction

Natural Causes

Extinction can happen in one place or in many places. Sometimes animals die out when people take over land and animals can no longer feed themselves. Other animals find it hard to reproduce. Many can't find enough food for their young. Other times, a small or weak species dies off when a stronger, larger species steals their **habitat.**

Big events such as wars, fires, or floods can kill species, too. A huge event called the Great Dying happened 250 million years ago. Scientists report that a volcano in Russia sent poisoned gas into the air. Ninety percent of all living species on Earth died. Those animals will never come back.

Natural disasters, like erupting volcanoes, can kill all the animals that made their homes in the area the disaster took place.

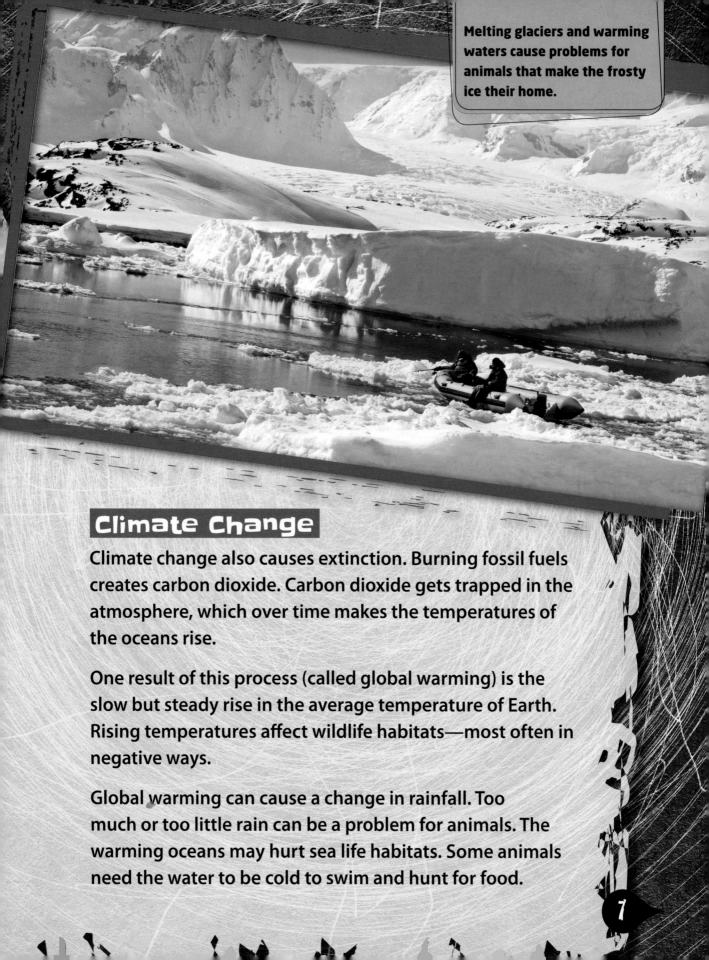

Melting glaciers and warming waters cause problems for animals that make the frosty ice their home.

Climate Change

Climate change also causes extinction. Burning fossil fuels creates carbon dioxide. Carbon dioxide gets trapped in the atmosphere, which over time makes the temperatures of the oceans rise.

One result of this process (called global warming) is the slow but steady rise in the average temperature of Earth. Rising temperatures affect wildlife habitats—most often in negative ways.

Global warming can cause a change in rainfall. Too much or too little rain can be a problem for animals. The warming oceans may hurt sea life habitats. Some animals need the water to be cold to swim and hunt for food.

Pollution from factories, cars, chemicals, and landfills can harm animals and environments. One cause of pollution is oil spills.

Oil spills can wipe out animal habitats. Spills also harm the animals themselves. In 1989, the oil tanker *Exxon Valdez* crashed in Alaska. About 11 million gallons (42 million l) of oil poured out, and it covered land and ocean all along the southern coast of Alaska. As a result of this one spill, a huge number of seabirds, otters, seals, and salmon died. It will take many years to bring back these species. Some may never recover.

Aquatic birds that get covered in oil after an oil spill are called "oiled birds." If they are not rescued, most will die. Oil spills in areas where aquatic birds are already endangered are especially damaging.

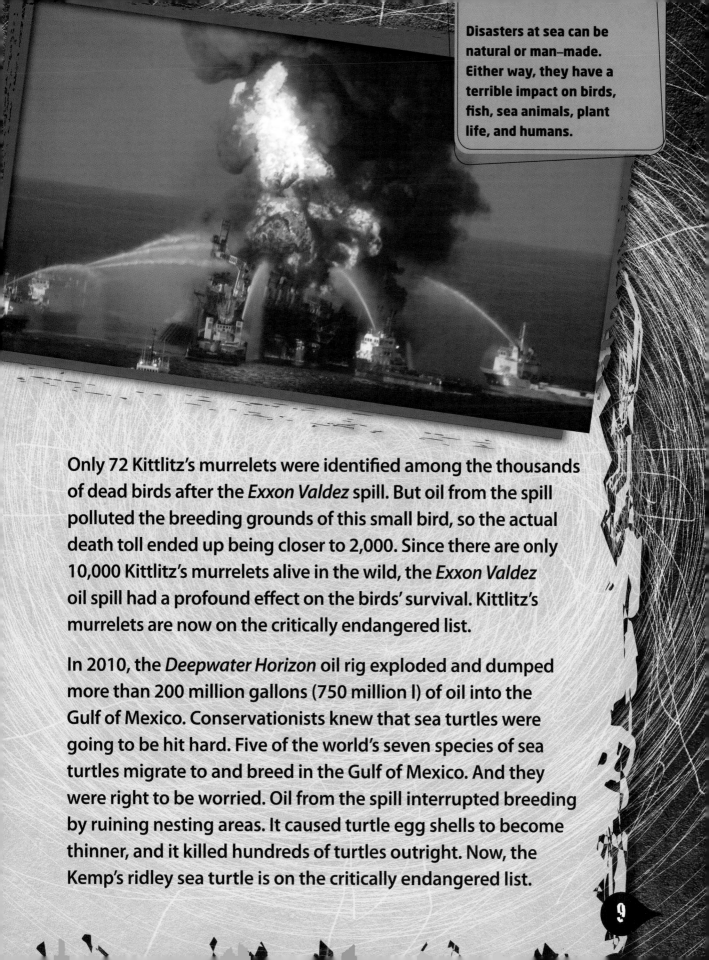

Disasters at sea can be natural or man–made. Either way, they have a terrible impact on birds, fish, sea animals, plant life, and humans.

Only 72 Kittlitz's murrelets were identified among the thousands of dead birds after the *Exxon Valdez* spill. But oil from the spill polluted the breeding grounds of this small bird, so the actual death toll ended up being closer to 2,000. Since there are only 10,000 Kittlitz's murrelets alive in the wild, the *Exxon Valdez* oil spill had a profound effect on the birds' survival. Kittlitz's murrelets are now on the critically endangered list.

In 2010, the *Deepwater Horizon* oil rig exploded and dumped more than 200 million gallons (750 million l) of oil into the Gulf of Mexico. Conservationists knew that sea turtles were going to be hit hard. Five of the world's seven species of sea turtles migrate to and breed in the Gulf of Mexico. And they were right to be worried. Oil from the spill interrupted breeding by ruining nesting areas. It caused turtle egg shells to become thinner, and it killed hundreds of turtles outright. Now, the Kemp's ridley sea turtle is on the critically endangered list.

Destruction of Habitat

Sometimes people destroy animal habitats by clearing the trees in a forest. First, workers cut or burn the trees. Then, they push the soil around with big earth-moving machines. Finally, they build farms, ranches, shopping centers, and businesses on the cleared land.

Animals that lived in these forests and on this land get scared. They don't know where to go and cannot find places to build nests for their babies. Many of the species will starve to death when their food source is gone, while others will escape and never return. This upsets the **ecosystem** and can lead to the extinction of a species.

Deforestation, or cutting down trees in a region, leads to loss of animal habitat and possible extinction of the animals that once lived here.

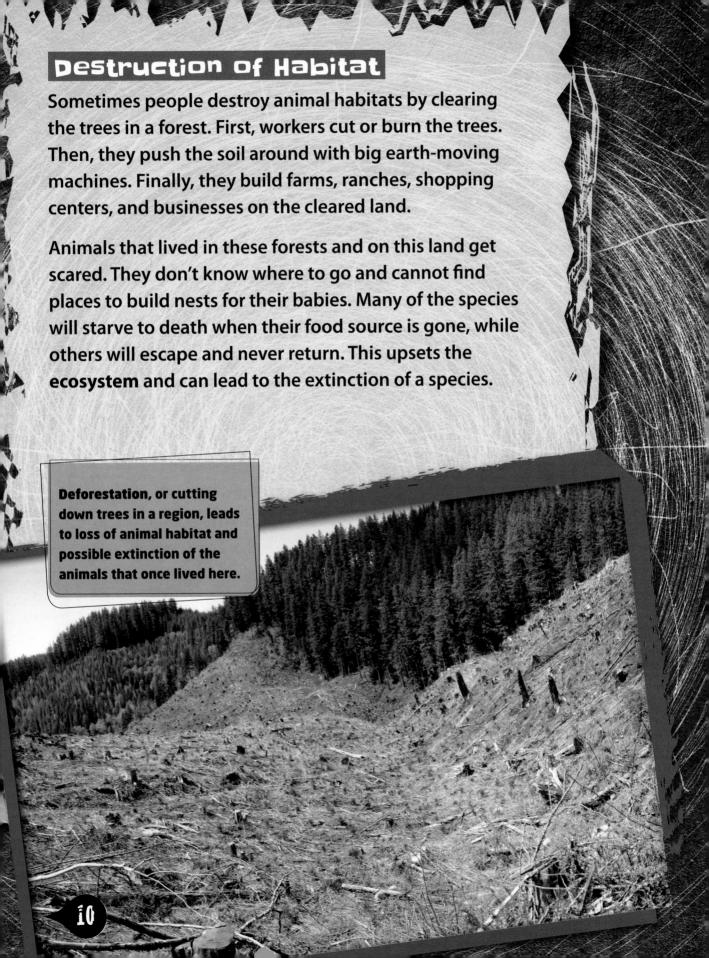

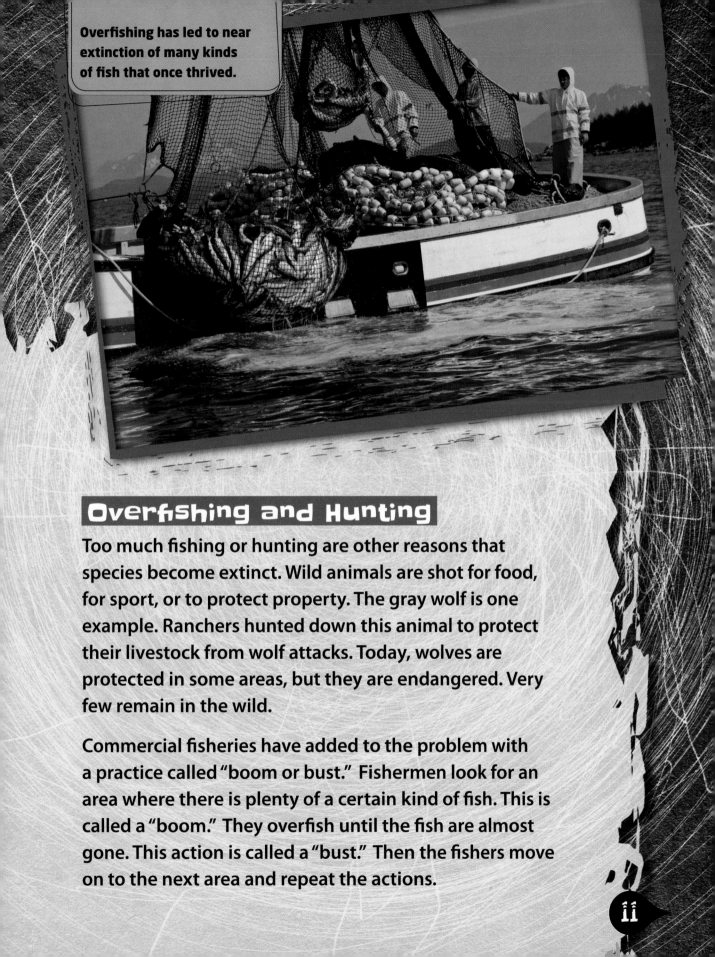

Overfishing has led to near extinction of many kinds of fish that once thrived.

Overfishing and Hunting

Too much fishing or hunting are other reasons that species become extinct. Wild animals are shot for food, for sport, or to protect property. The gray wolf is one example. Ranchers hunted down this animal to protect their livestock from wolf attacks. Today, wolves are protected in some areas, but they are endangered. Very few remain in the wild.

Commercial fisheries have added to the problem with a practice called "boom or bust." Fishermen look for an area where there is plenty of a certain kind of fish. This is called a "boom." They overfish until the fish are almost gone. This action is called a "bust." Then the fishers move on to the next area and repeat the actions.

Introduction of Invasive Species

Native species can go extinct when **invasive species** take over their habitats. Rats, for example, travel to new places on ships. They get loose and pass on disease to people and other animals. These animals can die from the new disease. House pets can also be a problem. They hunt some species to extinction. Pets can steal other animals' food and habitats.

In 1859, a man from England came to Australia with rabbits. He wanted to use them for hunting. The rabbit families grew fast. In 10 years, millions of rabbits ran all over the land. They ate everything they could find. Rabbits caused other species to go extinct in Australia. In 1907, authorities built a long fence to try to contain the rabbits.

Rabbits breed very quickly, eat a lot, and as a result, can force other species to abandon their natural habitats.

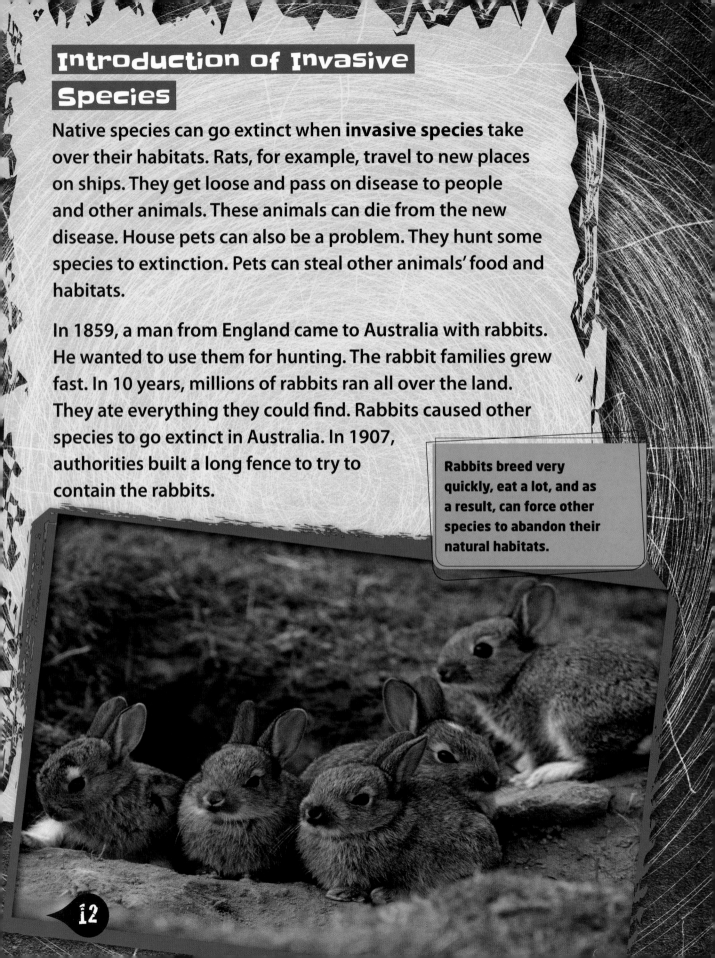

Golden parakeets are threatened by the animal trade. They are often taken illegally from their homes to become pets.

Animal Trade

Animal trade is a big problem for animals on the verge of extinction. It is against the law, but people break the law. They take tigers and parrots as pets. They steal snapping turtles for their shells and eggs. They shoot rhinos in South Africa for sport and for their horns. Hunters take the ivory tusks from elephants. In some countries, animal parts are used to make medicine.

Some animals die when captured. Others cannot reproduce. They come close to extinction when they are moved out of their habitat. Some people try to hide snakes, turtles, and golden parakeets in their clothing at airports in order to sell them as pets. Breaking the anti-trade laws hurts people, but it hurts the captured animals even more.

Consequences of Extinction

Destruction of Ecosystems

Should we care if some animals become extinct? Species come and go as a natural part of life. But yes, we should care. Many animals are close to extinction, and no other species can ever take their place.

Some species of animals cannot live away from each other. They work together to form an ecosystem. An ecosystem is a group of plants and animals living close together and helping each other. Sea snakes and many kinds of fish live together in the coral reefs in the oceans. Monkeys, toads, and birds live in the rainforest ecosystem. They depend upon each other and their environment to survive.

Tropical fish make their home in the warm waters of coral reefs. Together, the animals and their environment form an ecosystem.

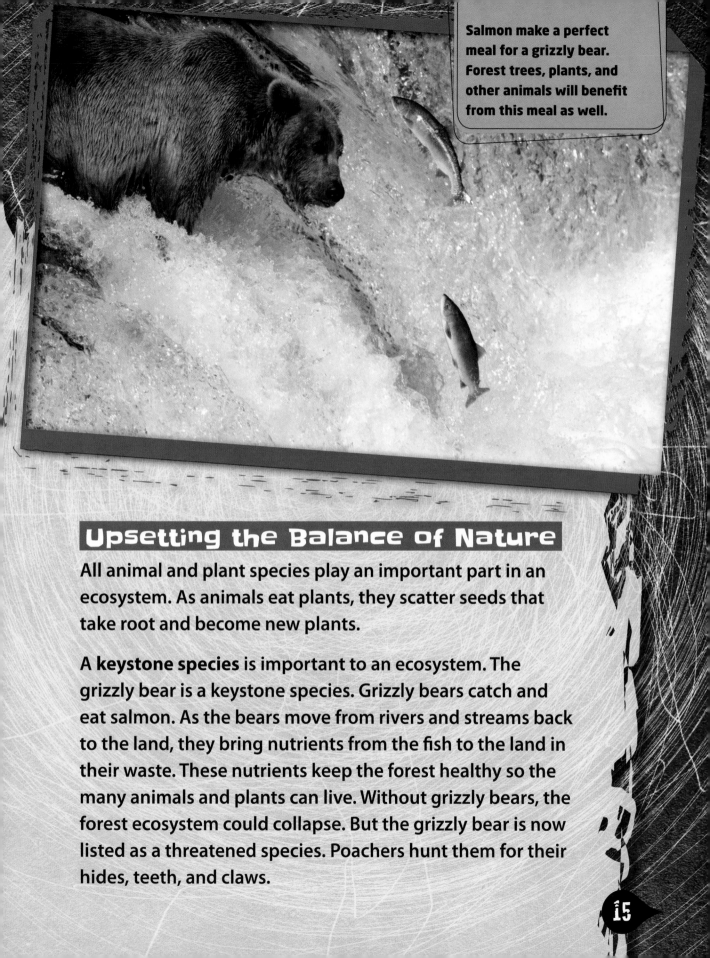

Salmon make a perfect meal for a grizzly bear. Forest trees, plants, and other animals will benefit from this meal as well.

Upsetting the Balance of Nature

All animal and plant species play an important part in an ecosystem. As animals eat plants, they scatter seeds that take root and become new plants.

A **keystone species** is important to an ecosystem. The grizzly bear is a keystone species. Grizzly bears catch and eat salmon. As the bears move from rivers and streams back to the land, they bring nutrients from the fish to the land in their waste. These nutrients keep the forest healthy so the many animals and plants can live. Without grizzly bears, the forest ecosystem could collapse. But the grizzly bear is now listed as a threatened species. Poachers hunt them for their hides, teeth, and claws.

Effects on Humans

When an animal species dies, people's lives change. Animals give us food and medicine. For instance, people around the world eat fish, but we have fished salmon and mussels to the verge of extinction.

Many of our medicines are made from plants and animals that live in the rainforest. But people are destroying these forests. This puts native species in danger.

Oil spills and environmental pollution cause species to die. They harm humans, too. People end up breathing polluted air or drinking polluted water. Thousands of people can lose fishing jobs when fish species go extinct. Extinction hurts all living things—people, plants, and animals.

Medicines can be made from plants in the rainforest. When rainforest plants go extinct before they have been studied, their uses cannot be discovered.

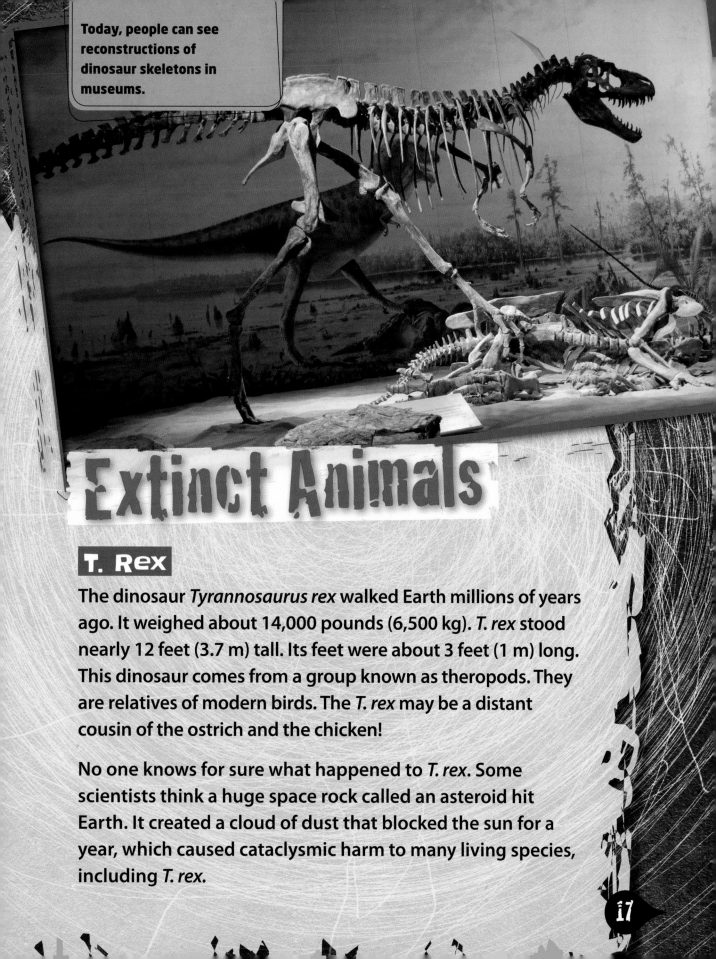

Today, people can see reconstructions of dinosaur skeletons in museums.

Extinct Animals

T. Rex

The dinosaur *Tyrannosaurus rex* walked Earth millions of years ago. It weighed about 14,000 pounds (6,500 kg). *T. rex* stood nearly 12 feet (3.7 m) tall. Its feet were about 3 feet (1 m) long. This dinosaur comes from a group known as theropods. They are relatives of modern birds. The *T. rex* may be a distant cousin of the ostrich and the chicken!

No one knows for sure what happened to *T. rex*. Some scientists think a huge space rock called an asteroid hit Earth. It created a cloud of dust that blocked the sun for a year, which caused cataclysmic harm to many living species, including *T. rex*.

Dodo

You may have heard the saying, "as dead as a dodo." The dodo bird once lived on an island in the Indian Ocean. Sailors in the 1600s stopped there for food and rest. They hunted the dodo for food. It took 100 years to drive the dodo to extinction.

Dodos probably ate fruit, nuts, and seeds. The dodos grew in number and in size because they had no predators. The birds also had plenty to eat. They became fat and their wings were too small to fly with bigger bodies. When the sailors hunted them, the dodos could not fly away.

Explorers and artists from Europe reported that the dodo was an odd-looking creature with a large head and huge beak. Today, these reports are all that is left of this gentle bird.

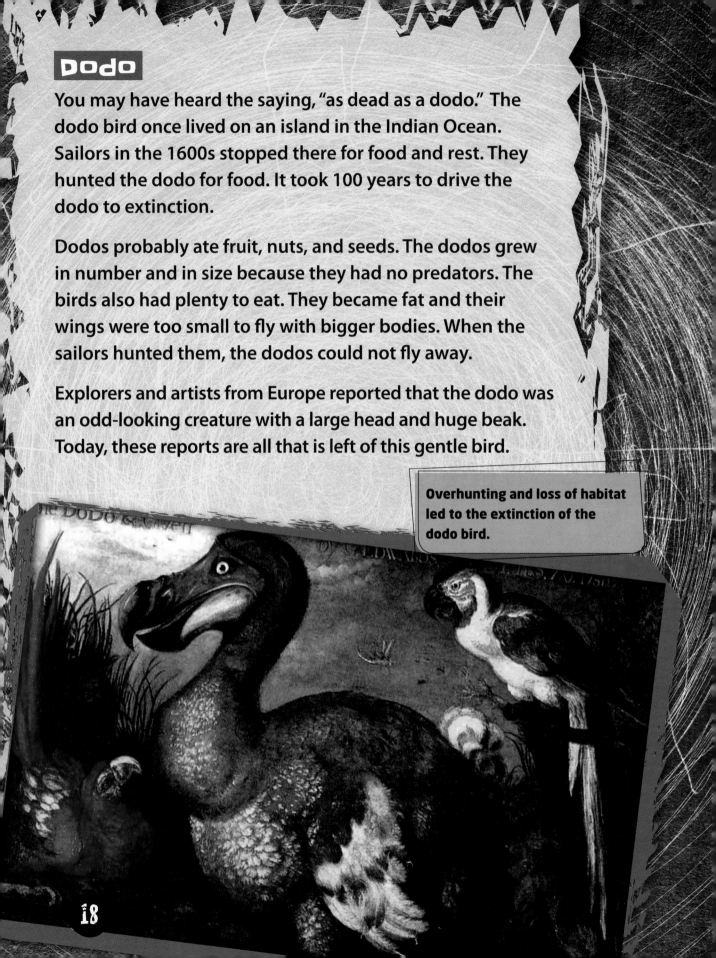

Overhunting and loss of habitat led to the extinction of the dodo bird.

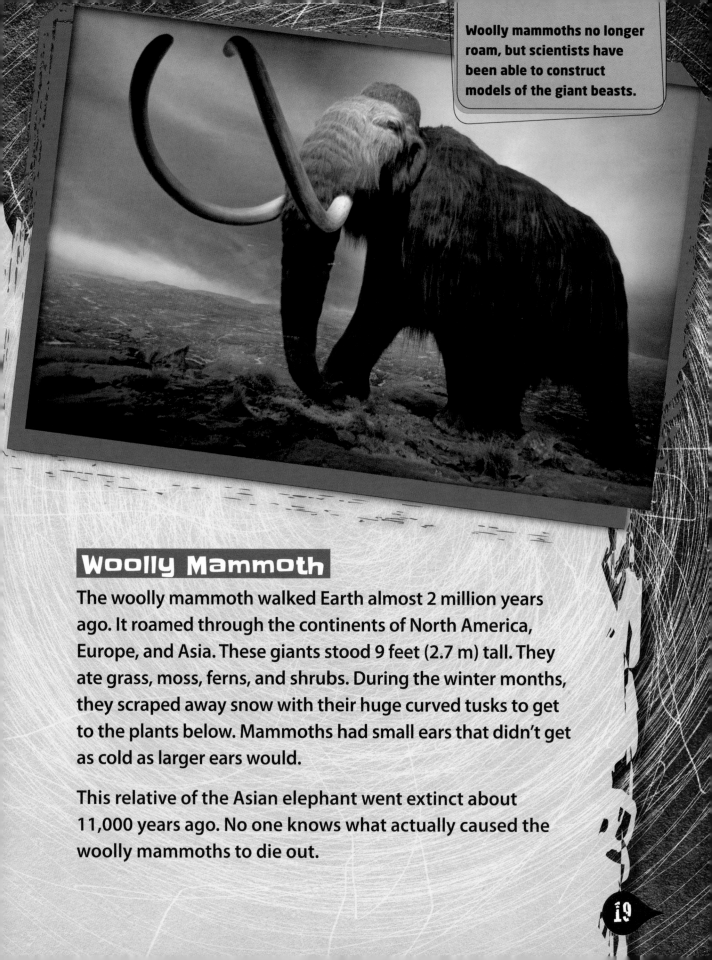

Woolly mammoths no longer roam, but scientists have been able to construct models of the giant beasts.

Woolly Mammoth

The woolly mammoth walked Earth almost 2 million years ago. It roamed through the continents of North America, Europe, and Asia. These giants stood 9 feet (2.7 m) tall. They ate grass, moss, ferns, and shrubs. During the winter months, they scraped away snow with their huge curved tusks to get to the plants below. Mammoths had small ears that didn't get as cold as larger ears would.

This relative of the Asian elephant went extinct about 11,000 years ago. No one knows what actually caused the woolly mammoths to die out.

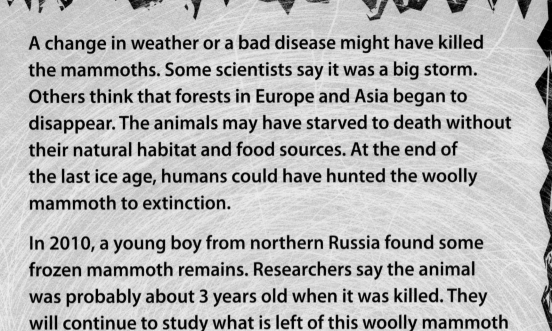

A change in weather or a bad disease might have killed the mammoths. Some scientists say it was a big storm. Others think that forests in Europe and Asia began to disappear. The animals may have starved to death without their natural habitat and food sources. At the end of the last ice age, humans could have hunted the woolly mammoth to extinction.

In 2010, a young boy from northern Russia found some frozen mammoth remains. Researchers say the animal was probably about 3 years old when it was killed. They will continue to study what is left of this woolly mammoth to see what can be learned about this species and the reasons for its disappearance.

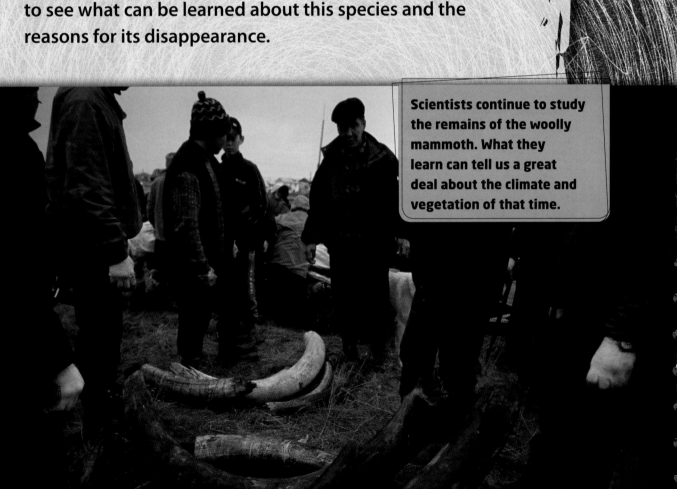

Scientists continue to study the remains of the woolly mammoth. What they learn can tell us a great deal about the climate and vegetation of that time.

While the Japanese sea lion has been hunted to extinction, other species of sea lions continue to thrive, and many are protected by laws.

Japanese Sea Lion

Japanese sea lions lived in the Sea of Japan for many years. Fishermen captured over 3,000 of these animals in the early 1900s. Thirty years later, fewer than 100 were left. More than 16,000 sea lions had been taken from the sea. The fishermen hunted this species to extinction.

The adult Japanese sea lions weighed about 1,000 pounds (450 kg). They were almost 9 feet (2.7 m) long. They ranged in color from light to dark gray. Females gave birth to their young on sandy beaches or in rocky areas. The rest of the time, Japanese sea lions lived in caves. No one knows why. Now it is too late to find out.

People hunted the sea lion for its skin and its fat, which is called blubber. They used the blubber to make oil. Sea lion whiskers made good pipe cleaners, and some people made clothes from the leather hides.

In early 1970, what was thought to be a young sea lion was found in the ocean near Japan. Researchers were excited. They hoped that there were still some Japanese sea lions alive. Unfortunately, it was a mistake. The animal they saw was a different species.

Captive sea lions can be taught to do many tricks. They perform in aquariums around the world.

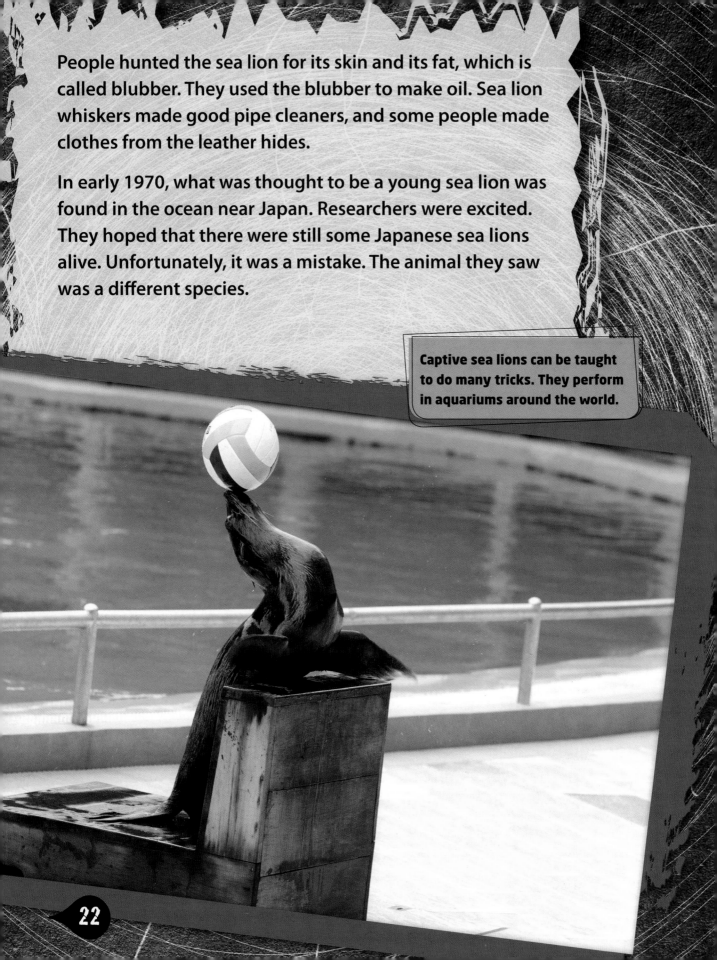

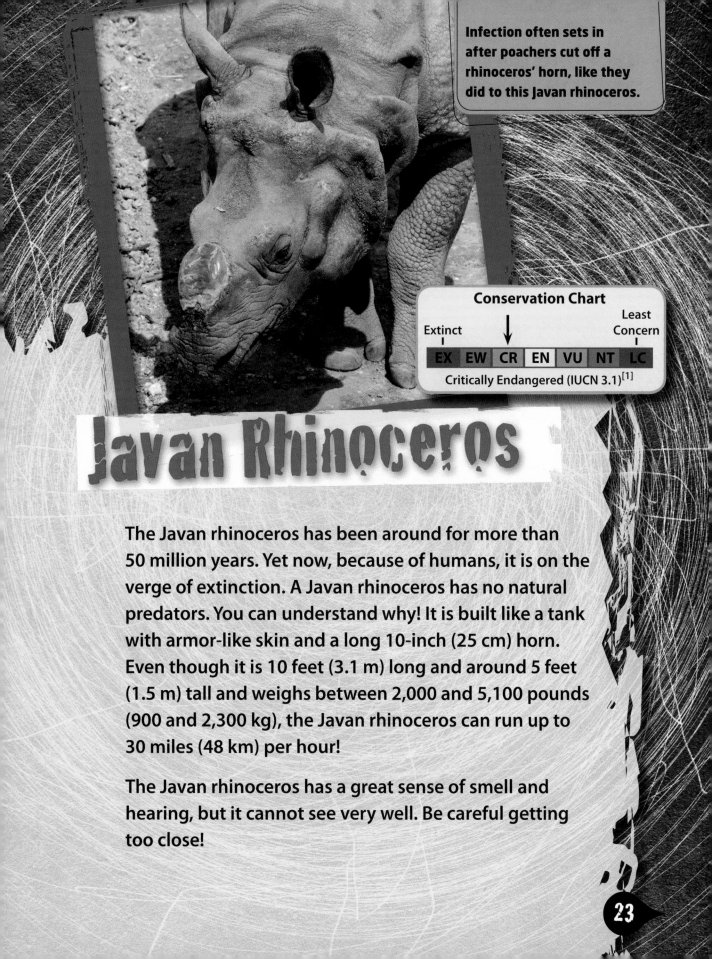

Infection often sets in after poachers cut off a rhinoceros' horn, like they did to this Javan rhinoceros.

Conservation Chart

Extinct → Least Concern

EX	EW	CR	EN	VU	NT	LC

Critically Endangered (IUCN 3.1)[1]

Javan Rhinoceros

The Javan rhinoceros has been around for more than 50 million years. Yet now, because of humans, it is on the verge of extinction. A Javan rhinoceros has no natural predators. You can understand why! It is built like a tank with armor-like skin and a long 10-inch (25 cm) horn. Even though it is 10 feet (3.1 m) long and around 5 feet (1.5 m) tall and weighs between 2,000 and 5,100 pounds (900 and 2,300 kg), the Javan rhinoceros can run up to 30 miles (48 km) per hour!

The Javan rhinoceros has a great sense of smell and hearing, but it cannot see very well. Be careful getting too close!

Java, a part of Indonesia, is the world's most populous island. Over 135 million people live on this island that is only 650 miles (1,050 km) long. Humans cut down forests to harvest wood. They also build roads, farms, and houses that crowd out the rhino's habitat. In the battle for land and resources, the Javan rhino is losing. Researchers think there are only 50 Javan rhinos alive in the world.

Loss of habitat is a big reason why this Asian one-horned rhinoceros struggles to find food and mates.

One huge threat to the survival of Javan rhinos like this one is poachers.

Another reason the Javan rhinoceros is critically endangered is that poachers—hunters who kill animals illegally—get paid a lot of money to kill the rhino for its horn. Some people, especially in Asia, think the horn of the rhino has special medicinal powers. They are wrong—it doesn't—but rhinos are slaughtered each year just the same.

If more is not done to protect the Javan rhinoceros, it will go extinct.

Ivory-Billed Woodpecker

Some animals on the verge of extinction may already be extinct. Such is the case with the ivory-billed woodpecker. Scientists have not moved North America's largest woodpecker from the critically endangered list to the extinct list because, very rarely, there are reported sightings of this interesting woodpecker.

At 20 inches (50 cm) long and with a wingspan of 30 inches (76 cm), the ivory-billed woodpecker lives—or lived—in the southeastern United States. The last sighting, which was not verified, was in 2004.

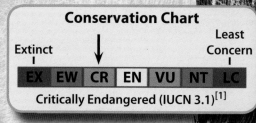

Conservation Chart

Extinct | ↓ | Least Concern

| EX | EW | CR | EN | VU | NT | LC |

Critically Endangered (IUCN 3.1)[1]

Sightings of the ivory-billed woodpecker are so rare that most conservationists have never seen one. They have to rely on drawings like this one.

In 2005, researchers thought they recorded the distinct "kent" call of the ivory-billed woodpecker—similar to the sound of a toy horn.

Why is the ivory-billed woodpecker critically endangered or extinct? There are two reasons. First, people hunted the bird for its unique feathers. At the same time, development and logging in the habitat where the woodpecker lived made it difficult for the bird to find food, mate, and raise its young.

Although microphones planted in a gorge like this one captured what some hoped to be the distinct "kent" call of the ivory-billed woodpecker in 2005, the last verified recording of this bird is from 1935. The ivory-billed woodpecker shows how difficult it is to determine if a species is actually extinct or not.

So rare are sightings of the ivory-billed woodpecker that in 2008, the Cornell Lab of Ornithology offered a $5,000 reward to anyone who could locate a living ivory-billed woodpecker. No one has stepped forward to claim the reward.

This illustration done in 1878 captures the ivory-billed woodpecker's magnificent size. It is (or was) a very large woodpecker.

This picture shows whalers skinning a North Pacific right whale. Whalers targeted the North Pacific right whale because it was full of oil-rich blubber, and it was easy to hunt and kill.

Conservation Chart

Extinct → Least Concern

| EX | EW | CR | EN | VU | NT | LC |

Endangered (IUCN 3.1)[2]

North Pacific Right Whale

The North Pacific right whale got its name for all the wrong reasons. Whalers named it the "right" whale because it was easy to kill!

Like all whales, the North Pacific right whale is massive in a scale that is almost beyond description. Adults are about 50 feet (15 m) long and can weigh up to 70 tons (63,500 kg). Their tongues weigh as much as an elephant!

But for all its massive size, the North Pacific right whale was surprisingly susceptible to being hunted by whalers. For one thing, this giant mammal is a "skimmer;" it skims the surface of the water for **krill** and plankton. Another reason whalers hunted this whale was because it was full of blubber and precious oil. Plus, it floated after it was killed, making it easier to handle.

Before the fleets of whaling ships hunted them down, there were more than 20,000 North Pacific right whales. Now, there may be fewer than 50 left. Even though the North Pacific right whale is protected by international laws, some are killed each year when they get caught up in commercial fishing nets.

The North Pacific right whale, because of extensive whaling, is now almost extinct.

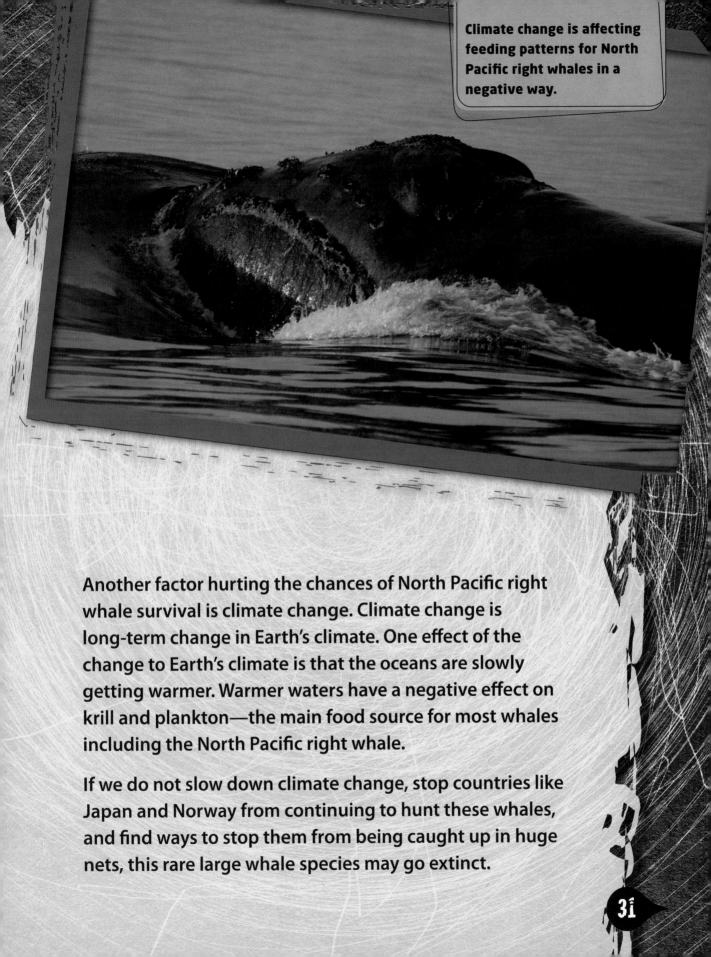

Climate change is affecting feeding patterns for North Pacific right whales in a negative way.

Another factor hurting the chances of North Pacific right whale survival is climate change. Climate change is long-term change in Earth's climate. One effect of the change to Earth's climate is that the oceans are slowly getting warmer. Warmer waters have a negative effect on krill and plankton—the main food source for most whales including the North Pacific right whale.

If we do not slow down climate change, stop countries like Japan and Norway from continuing to hunt these whales, and find ways to stop them from being caught up in huge nets, this rare large whale species may go extinct.

Asian Elephant

It's hard to imagine that a beast that stands 9 feet (2.7 m) tall and weighs 6,000 pounds (2,720 kg) can be threatened by anything. But the largest land animal in all of Asia—the Asian elephant—is endangered.

Experts estimate that there are fewer than 40,000 Asian elephants alive today. That may sound like a big number until you realize that there were 10 times that number 100 years ago.

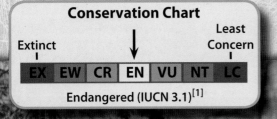

Conservation Chart

Extinct

Least Concern

| EX | EW | CR | EN | VU | NT | LC |

Endangered (IUCN 3.1)[1]

Hunters sometime kill elephants just for their tusks. Other times hunters cut off the tusks, leaving the elephant injured and with no way to defend itself or dig for food.

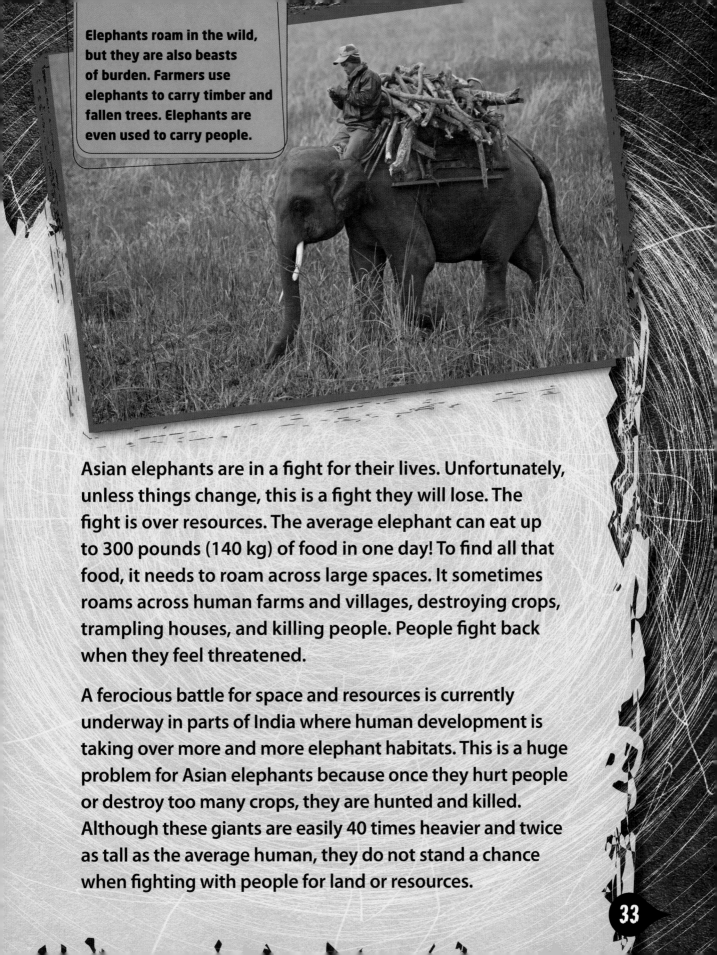

Elephants roam in the wild, but they are also beasts of burden. Farmers use elephants to carry timber and fallen trees. Elephants are even used to carry people.

Asian elephants are in a fight for their lives. Unfortunately, unless things change, this is a fight they will lose. The fight is over resources. The average elephant can eat up to 300 pounds (140 kg) of food in one day! To find all that food, it needs to roam across large spaces. It sometimes roams across human farms and villages, destroying crops, trampling houses, and killing people. People fight back when they feel threatened.

A ferocious battle for space and resources is currently underway in parts of India where human development is taking over more and more elephant habitats. This is a huge problem for Asian elephants because once they hurt people or destroy too many crops, they are hunted and killed. Although these giants are easily 40 times heavier and twice as tall as the average human, they do not stand a chance when fighting with people for land or resources.

Asian elephants follow migratory patterns. When humans build roads, farms, and houses in the wild, they cut off the elephants from these ancient routes. The elephant herds become fragmented and isolated.

Another threat to Asian elephants is poachers who kill elephants just for the ivory in their tusks. In 1975, it became illegal to buy or sell ivory taken from Asian elephants, but that has not stopped poachers from killing hundreds each year.

Female elephants stay together, and they are very protective of their little ones.

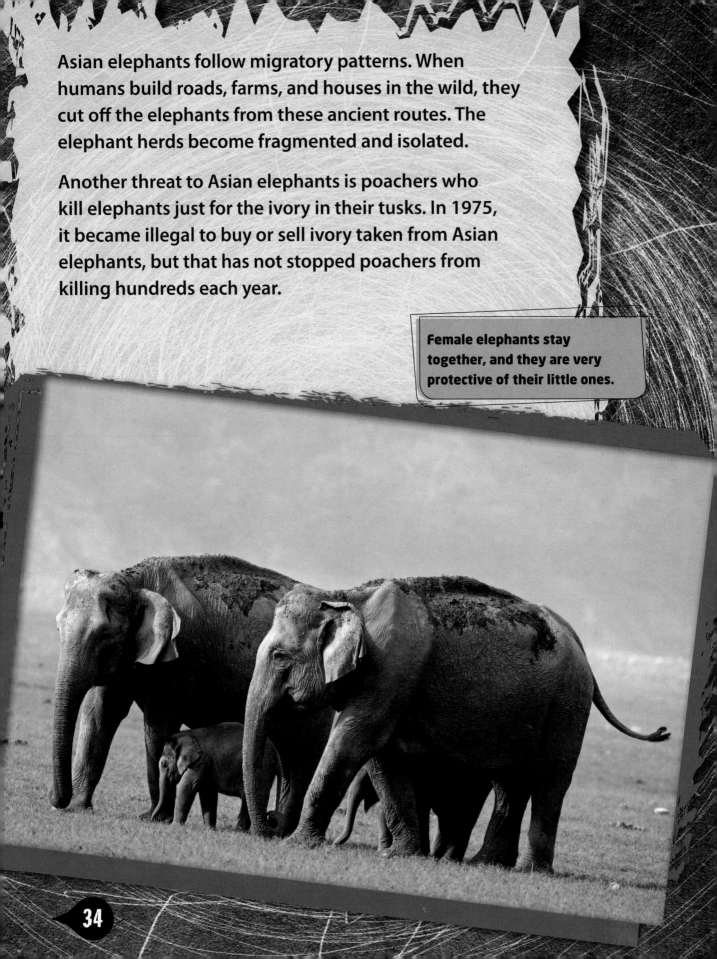

Overfishing has decimated the southern bluefin tuna. Very few are left in the wild.

Southern Bluefin Tuna

Conservation Chart

Extinct			↓			Least Concern
EX	EW	CR	EN	VU	NT	LC

Critically Endangered (IUCN 3.1)[1]

Most of us have eaten tuna sandwiches. But one kind of tuna, southern bluefin tuna, is on the verge of extinction in the wild. Fishermen have caught so many in the last 50 years that this species is almost gone. The number of tuna left is below 5 percent of what it used to be. Scientists now list the southern bluefin tuna as endangered.

Why has this happened? Money is the short answer. Just one southern bluefin tuna can sell for more than $100,000. So, pirate fishermen catch the tuna and sell it. In addition, some commercial fishermen catch more than the law allows.

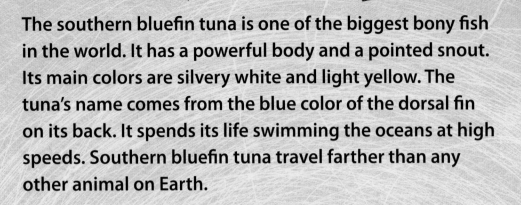

The southern bluefin tuna is one of the biggest bony fish in the world. It has a powerful body and a pointed snout. Its main colors are silvery white and light yellow. The tuna's name comes from the blue color of the dorsal fin on its back. It spends its life swimming the oceans at high speeds. Southern bluefin tuna travel farther than any other animal on Earth.

This fish lays its eggs only in the Indian Ocean. Then it swims the seas in the southern half of Earth. Tuna fishermen in Australia send out "spotter" planes to find the fish.

A sports fishermen tries to grab a southern bluefin tuna he's caught in a large net.

Young bluefin tuna are netted and trapped alive, only to be fattened up and then served as sushi.

Over 4,500 tons (4 million kg) of tuna are brought in every year. Most of these fish are young. They are put into sea cages and given a lot of food. This fattens them up, and then they are shipped to Japan. The southern bluefin tuna meat is delicious, and sushi restaurants buy large amounts. Japanese and western chefs say it is the best-tasting raw fish in the world. While that may be true, very few people believe it is worth driving the species into extinction.

Mountain Gorilla

It may seem hard to believe that an animal as massive and strong as the mountain gorilla is also on the verge of extinction, but it is.

Although huge and immensely powerful, mountain gorillas are peaceful, social animals. They spend most of their time sleeping, hunting for food, and socializing within the troop. Males are extremely protective. The leader, called a silverback, will pound its chest or charge a stranger if it feels threatened. It will fight to the death to protect its troop.

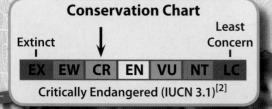

Conservation Chart

Extinct						Least Concern
EX	EW	CR	EN	VU	NT	LC

Critically Endangered (IUCN 3.1)[2]

A peaceful mother and her young curl up for a midday snooze.

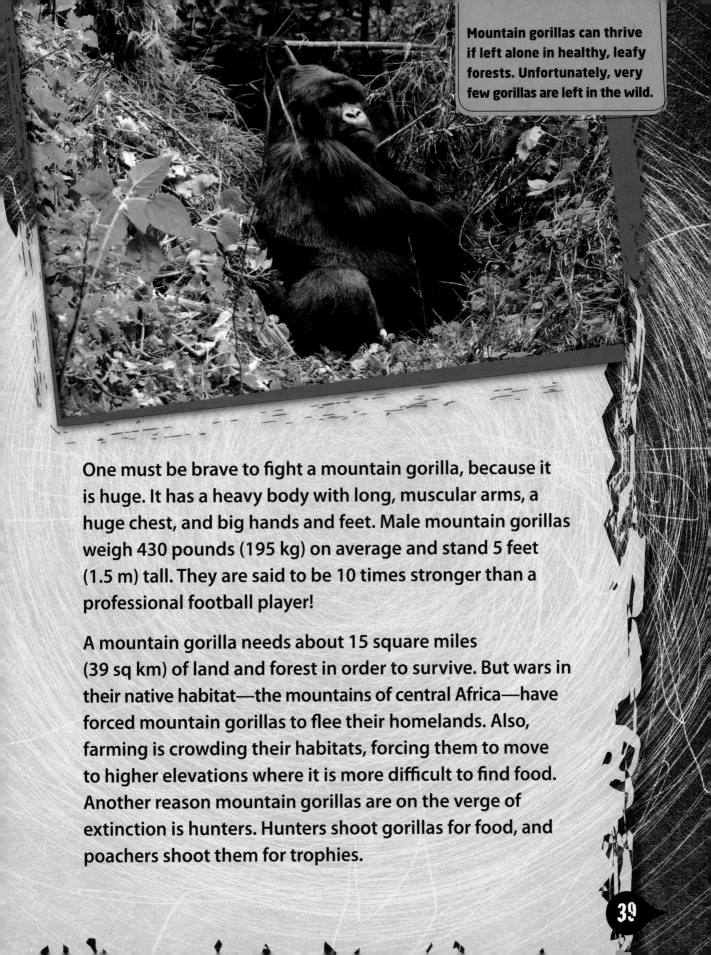

Mountain gorillas can thrive if left alone in healthy, leafy forests. Unfortunately, very few gorillas are left in the wild.

One must be brave to fight a mountain gorilla, because it is huge. It has a heavy body with long, muscular arms, a huge chest, and big hands and feet. Male mountain gorillas weigh 430 pounds (195 kg) on average and stand 5 feet (1.5 m) tall. They are said to be 10 times stronger than a professional football player!

A mountain gorilla needs about 15 square miles (39 sq km) of land and forest in order to survive. But wars in their native habitat—the mountains of central Africa—have forced mountain gorillas to flee their homelands. Also, farming is crowding their habitats, forcing them to move to higher elevations where it is more difficult to find food. Another reason mountain gorillas are on the verge of extinction is hunters. Hunters shoot gorillas for food, and poachers shoot them for trophies.

Finally, a virus deadly to mountain gorillas has ravaged them. Some scientists say that the virus has killed up to 5,000 mountain gorillas.

The mountain gorilla was not even known to science until 1902. However, just over 100 years later, there are fewer than 800 left. If more is not done to protect them, mountain gorillas will become extinct.

A silverback gorilla can weigh nearly 500 pounds (230 kg). Although they are big, they are also shy.

Loss of habitat is one reason leatherback sea turtles like this one are on the verge of extinction.

Conservation Chart

Extinct			↓			Least Concern
EX	EW	CR	EN	VU	NT	LC

Critically Endangered (IUCN 3.1)[1]

Leatherback Sea Turtle

The world's largest turtle is also one of the most endangered. In fact, the International Union for Conservation of Nature lists it as critically endangered. In 1980, there were 115,000. Today, there are less than 30,000.

Leatherbacks measure up to 6 feet (1.8 m) long and 4 feet (1.2 m) wide and weigh up to 880 pounds (400 kg). The easiest way to identify a leatherback sea turtle is that it does not have a bony shell. Instead, its back is covered by hard, leathery skin.

The world's biggest turtle is also its best swimmer. The leatherback swims all over the globe. It hatches on a beach in Japan and then swims 7,500 miles (12,000 km) to Baja, California. The male leatherback spends its entire life at sea.

When the female leatherback is ready to lay her eggs, she returns to the same beach where she was hatched, digs a hole, and lays her eggs. A single female can lay between 100 and 150 eggs at one time. That is a lot of eggs! Unfortunately, most do not live to adulthood. Leatherback sea turtle eggs and baby turtles are a favorite food for many animals including raccoons, seabirds, and sharks. Turtle soup is in great demand in many parts of Asia.

This leatherback sea turtle is laying her eggs on a beach in Trinidad.

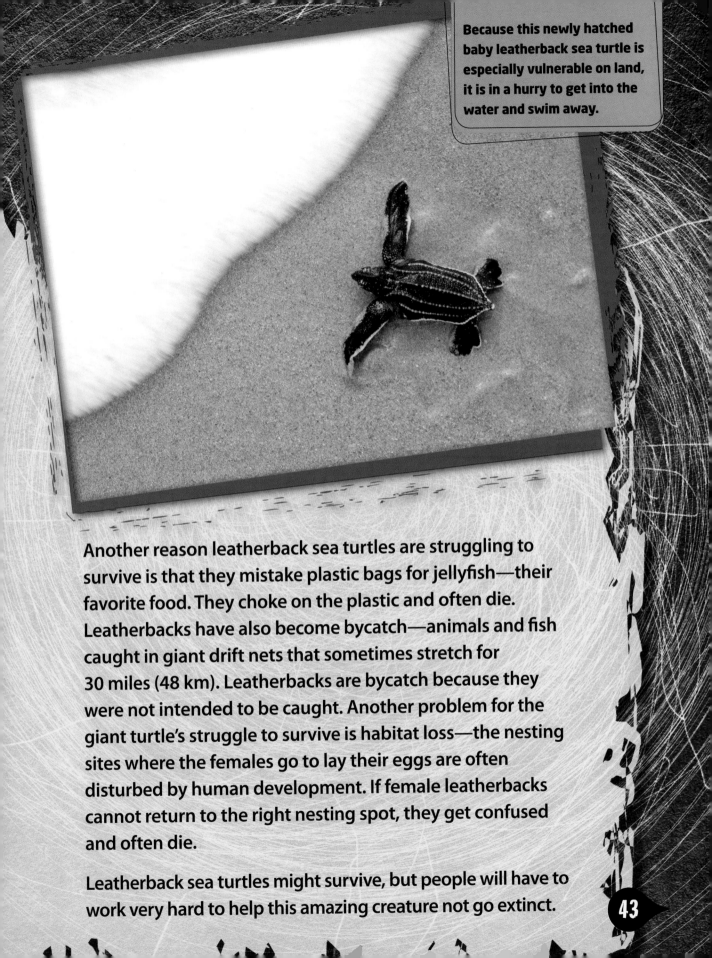

Because this newly hatched baby leatherback sea turtle is especially vulnerable on land, it is in a hurry to get into the water and swim away.

Another reason leatherback sea turtles are struggling to survive is that they mistake plastic bags for jellyfish—their favorite food. They choke on the plastic and often die. Leatherbacks have also become bycatch—animals and fish caught in giant drift nets that sometimes stretch for 30 miles (48 km). Leatherbacks are bycatch because they were not intended to be caught. Another problem for the giant turtle's struggle to survive is habitat loss—the nesting sites where the females go to lay their eggs are often disturbed by human development. If female leatherbacks cannot return to the right nesting spot, they get confused and often die.

Leatherback sea turtles might survive, but people will have to work very hard to help this amazing creature not go extinct.

Conservation Efforts

Although the situation regarding animals on the verge of extinction is grim, there are some signs of hope.

The International Union for Conservation of Nature (IUCN) has a global network of conservationists who track and monitor endangered species. The United States passed the Endangered Species Act which makes it illegal to trap, kill, or sell an endangered species. It is now illegal to buy or sell ivory taken from Asian elephants.

Many countries have set apart protected areas of land called preserves where endangered animals can live and be safe. The Arctic National Wildlife Refuge is home to caribou, polar bears, grizzly bears, musk ox, wolves, and many other species. Uganda, Rwanda, and the Democratic Republic of Congo all have created national parks to protect their gorillas.

Wildlife preserves provide a safe home for animals to live, eat, and raise their young. Visitors can also come to see animals in their native habitats.

These are all good steps. But much more needs to be done to not just slow, but also reverse the problems leading to so many animals being on the verge of extinction. For once one of these beautiful, amazing, complex creatures goes extinct, it will never come back.

In captive breeding programs, workers help care for mother and baby animals, like these in a national park.

Glossary

captive breeding: the process of breeding animals in human–controlled environments

carnivorous: meat or flesh eating

deforestation: the result of converting forested areas to nonforested areas

ecosystem: a community of living things and the surroundings in which they live

endangered: in danger of dying out within 20 years

extinct: no longer existing

extirpation: to becoming extinct in one area

habitat: the surroundings where an animal or a plant naturally lives

invasive species: a plant or animal that is not native to the ecosystem and whose introduction causes or is likely to cause economic or environmental harm

keystone species: species whose presence and role within an ecosystem has a disproportionate effect on other organisms within the system

krill: small marine crustaceans that are the principal food of baleen whales

species: a single kind of living thing

For More Information

Books

Bonneville, Patrick. *Humanity: Threatened: 100 Species on the Verge of Extinction*. Sutton, Quebec: Patrick Bonneville Society, 2010.

Weston, Chris. *Animals on the Edge: Reporting from the Frontline of Extinction*. New York: Thames & Hudson, 2009.

Websites

International Union for Conservation of Nature
www.iucn.org
The IUCN website acts as a clearinghouse for all things conservation, including information about wildlife threatened by extinction.

World Wildlife Fund
worldwildlife.org/
WWF works in 100 countries to promote wildlife conservation and preservation.

Index